Musical Common Sense

For Keyboardists

By: Khadijah SImon

Acknowledgments

Firstly, I would like to thank my parents, Pauline Richards-Simon and Steve Simon, for being supportive of my musical aspirations since day one.

To my classical piano teacher, Ms. Louise Joseph, thank you for finding the balance between teaching me what I needed to know and giving me the space to explore whatever I wanted. You never shunned me from doing things that were "unusual," which taught me from an early age that there are no barriers to what I can do musically.

To my dearest "Uncle" Bruce (Bruce Skerritt), who was the inspiration behind writing this book, thank you for changing my mindset towards music completely, allowing me to be more creative, curious, and mindful. Your teachings live on in this book, in me, and in the countless others you have touched. This one is for you!

Many thanks to Shaeil Mayers for assisting me with the book's design, serving as a proofreader, and a dedicated sounding board. You are the greatest.

Lastly, I want to thank my friends and musical influences worldwide who have also inspired me during my ongoing quest to understand the inner workings of music.

Harry Likas, Arturo Tappin, Andrew Dorsett, Kimdale Mackellar, Dr. George Roberts, Jesse Ryan, Winston Bailey, and others who are too numerous to mention!

Your consistent support, advice, and inspiration have impacted me greatly, and I am immensely grateful.

Table Of Contents

Acknowledgments 2
Table Of Contents 4
How To Get The Most Out Of This Book 5
Chapter 1: Initial Thoughts 6
Chapter 2: In Theory 9
Chapter 3: In Action 13
Chapter 4: Staying Fit 18
Chapter 5: Do This For Yourself 22
Chapter 6: Your New Musical Philosophy 25
Extra letters 30
    On Classical Study (Khadijah Simon) 31
    Playing What You Hear (Bruce Skerritt) 33
    Rehearsal vs. Practice (Khadijah Simon) 35
    Playing music "by ear" (Bruce Skerritt) 36
    Mastery Is A Hoax (Khadijah Simon) 37
    What Does Practice Make? (Khadijah Simon) 39
    The Music Spirit (Khadijah Simon) 41
    The Vessel Mindset (Khadijah Simon) 42
    Why Is It So Hard To Improvise? (Khadijah Simon) 43

How To Get The Most Out Of This Book

To get the most use out of this book, it is recommended that you read each tip and essay with an open mind, taking as much time as you need to think about how you can apply it to your musical endeavors.

Some concepts will register instantly, but others may take a bit longer to give you that lightbulb effect. There is nothing wrong with this. Just be patient with yourself!

If any tips sound vague to you, keep reading and meditating on them. The meaning will come to you eventually, and when it does, you will hear and feel the difference!

All in all, patience and critical thinking is key. Make notes, experiment, and do research if you need to. It will only benefit YOU!

Chapter 1: Initial Thoughts

Upright piano at Princeton University, Photo Credit: Khadijah Simon

"Musical common sense" is probably not a term you've heard of before. I never heard of it either until the phrase popped up in my head one day.

As musicians, there's a certain level of know-how we should possess to be able to function effectively in whatever musical situation we're placed in.

You can easily see and hear the differences between the people who know these things and the ones who don't.

My goal is to decrease the number of people who aren't in the know.

This book is not just a list of tips; it is a powerful tool that can be used to build a mindset, so it is my only wish that you treat it as such.

1. Your first instruments are voice and percussion. Craft your melodies with this in mind.

2. Good rhythm is more important than good notes. Always strive to have good rhythm.

3. To be a great keyboard player, you MUST be a great musician. Anybody can play a keyboard, but only musicians can play music.

4. Be open-minded in music and life. An open mind is an open vessel.

5. Understand that you will never stop learning.

6. Learn other instruments. They all help each other out.

7. Voice leading is crucial. You are responsible for every note you play and ALL of them need somewhere to go.

8. Play ideas, not scales or licks. Scales and licks should be tools used to help you formulate your IDEAS.

9. If you're unable to play what you hear in your head, fix it. "How do you fix it?" Take some time to sit down, listen to what is in your head, and then work it out slowly.

10. You must take time to explore your instrument. Mindful exploration can turn into significant discovery.

11. You can not be upset about not progressing if you do not take time out to practice!

12. The only thing more important than notes in music is the silence between them.

Chapter 2: In Theory

Jackson Bettencourt (Bruce's grandson) at the piano with company.

There are thousands of books that teach theory, but very few teach the common sense that needs to go with applying it.

We seem to have developed a worldwide issue with musicians who are only playing certain things because a theory book says it should be okay. There is little to no consideration about why, or if it sounds good or not.

Many musicians don't know how to apply the concepts they learn, and this greatly affects the quality of the music.

13. "Rules" in music exist to help you. When you're just starting out, rules are your framework. As you gain more experience, they become your guide.

14. Do not disregard the accidentals of the key that you're playing in.

15. Learn how to read and write chord charts.

16. Do not take any gigs until you understand the Nashville Number System.

17. Why play a 2-5 when you can put them together? Welcome to the world of sus chords. 2 on the top and 5 on the bottom!

18. The only difference between a minor 6th chord and a half-diminished chord is an inversion.

19. The only difference between a major 6th chord and a minor 7th chord is an inversion.

20. The blues and pentatonic scales should be assets to your improvisation, not crutches.

21. A whole-half diminished scale is a minor scale tetrachord, plus the tetrachord of the minor scale that is a tritone above the root of your first tetrachord.

22. The chord that a song starts isn't always the key that the song is in.

23. Think of diminished scales as one scale with 2 modes: whole-half (WH) and half-whole (HW).
C whole-half will end up being D half-whole if you play the C whole-half diminished scale starting on D.

24. If you're playing a minor 7b5 chord, a natural 5 has no place in it.

25. There are only 3 different diminished chords/scales, and 2 different whole-tone scales. Don't waste time learning 12.

26. Once a 7th chord doesn't specify what quality it is, it is a dominant 7 chord.

27. Upper structures create beautiful tension; when voice-lead properly. Good voice-leading is KEY. Always remember that.

28. They say that if you like how something sounds, it is right. I say some people may have bad taste. Don't have bad taste.

29. Improvising is easier than you think. Forget scales and licks. Think of melodies that fit over the changes. The scales and licks will come out but in melody form. There's a difference.

30. Harmonizing IS NOT just playing/singing a melody in thirds.

Chapter 3: In Action

Khadijah Simon and Mind Sound live at Julees in Antigua

It's time to get on the bandstand. You can either make the people you're playing with like you or dislike you. It all depends on how and what you play.

Depending on what kind of situation you're in, you may have to play a part that isn't piano. Maybe it's a horn part. Maybe it's a guitar riff or maybe it's a flute part. You HAVE to know what the instrument's limitations are in order to play these parts as authentically as possible.

Think of yourself as a guitar player or a horn player and mimic how they'd play their instrument using yours.

Whether you acknowledge it or not, how you play something makes a big difference!

31. If your technique gets the job done without injury or strain, then it is right for you. Music is not one-size-fits-all in any sense of the word.

32. "Correct" fingering is not very important. Playing the notes comfortably is (emphasis on comfortably). A crowd isn't watching to see how you fingered your diminished scale.

33. Repetition can legitimize but it can also boring-ize.

34. You have to be extra sensitive when you're accompanying someone.

35. In a band setting, you need to pay attention to what's going on around you musically. You are not playing by yourself!

36. If your bassist knows more turnarounds than you, it's time to hit the shed.

37. When playing by yourself, the melody is king. Don't lose it. If you lose the melody, you lose the song.

38. Be aware of your voicings, and what notes you allow to ring out. Practice allowing different notes to ring out.

39. Some songs don't need fancy reharmonizations and chord extensions.

40. There is a feeling in between straight and swung. I call it bounce. This makes your music feel good. Play right inside of that bounce.

41. If you're playing different instrument sounds on your keyboard, be realistic. Guitars can't play more than 6 notes at a time, and a solo trumpet CAN NOT harmonize with itself.

42. Don't get in the way of anyone you're playing with. You wouldn't want them to get in yours.

43. Pay attention to the skill level of the people that you play with. If they don't know as much as you, don't play over their heads. They won't be able to find what you're doing and the music will suffer.

44. Don't dwell on mistakes. The truth is, that mistakes will never stop. Learn how to recover from them.

45. In a band setting, the bass player determines the root of a chord. Don't try to compete!

46. If you play something once, play it again. Make it even. Not every phrase wants to be lonely.

47. Being able to play fast is cool, but being able to play in the pocket is way cooler.

48. If you have to play a horn line, do it just a little behind the beat. Horn players can't be quantized.

49. Ending every song with a major 7th chord is cheesy. Sometimes all a song calls for is a plain old triad, or a dominant 7#9 if you're feeling funky!

50. If you don't feel it, don't play it.

51. Every instrument has a pocket. Know when to stay and leave yours.

52. Every genre has its nuances. To play them well, learn the nuances.

53. Learn to hear and understand the difference between "straight" and "swung".

54. A keyboard player can give you as many tips as they can about your role in a band, but only the other musicians in the band (bassist, drummer, guitarist) can show you what your role looks like.

Chapter 4: Staying Fit

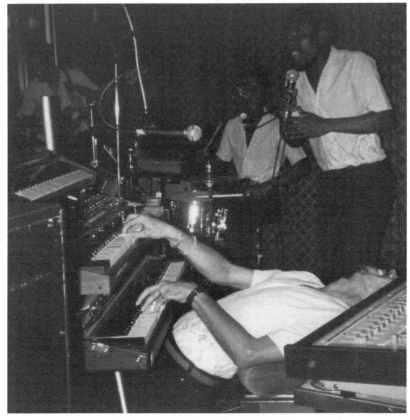

Bruce Skerritt "letting loose" with a band

What does staying fit have to do with playing music? More than you think!

Have you ever tried lugging a 30-pound keyboard from your car to the bandstand? Or tried to stand up and play for 3 hours straight!

Simply put, being a musician is taxing, and the only way to counteract that is to be as healthy as possible and ready to face whatever comes your way!

Aside from physical fitness, there is also an equally important need for musical fitness. You have to keep your chops up to date or else they will leave you.

You have to keep learning the theory, keep practicing, and keep analyzing the music.

55. You are an empty vessel before the music enters. The quality of the music that enters depends on how you upkeep your vessel.

56. Make it a priority to stay fit musically, physically, and spiritually.

57. Don't just learn piano licks, learn bass licks, learn trumpet licks- hell, learn drum licks!

58. No hand is more important than the other. They're both necessary. Put the same effort into both hands when practicing.

59. Don't run away from challenging pieces. Tackle them head-on.

60. Play with musicians that send you home to practice.

61. Do not overwork yourself. Take some time off to recharge if you need to.

62. When you feel tired of playing, start listening.

63. Marinate yourself in the music you want to play by listening to it as much as you can. Sometimes this is just as effective as practicing.

64. Do wrist strengthening exercises before you play and read books about playing with good technique. Get a teacher if you need to!

65. There's a lot of talk about hand independence but not so much about finger independence. Make finger independence a priority. Assign tasks to each finger when you play. Split your fingers into parts.

66. Learn a new song every week. The more music you know, the more material you have to experiment with.

67. It is not how long you practice, it's WHAT you practice.

Chapter 5: Do This For Yourself

Bruce Skerritt behind the keyboard.

As a musician, your duties aren't just limited to playing an instrument. Sometimes you will have to be your own sales and marketing rep, an instrument repair tech, or even an amateur singer.

It is important to have knowledge in these fields because these situations are inevitable.
Sometimes a cable might have a strange buzz, or your instrument may not be making any sound.

You need to be able to identify what is making this happen and how it can be fixed. Who knows? If you become competent enough, you can offer your expertise to other people as an additional source of income.

68. Learn how your gear works and how to do basic repairs/troubleshooting.

69. Take the time to educate yourself about the business side of music. That includes marketing, sales, and all the legal stuff. You don't want to get taken advantage of by someone who knows more than you.

70. Always be punctual. Try to arrive at your gig at least an hour before it starts, and make sure you always have extra cables, pedals, in-ears, etc.

71. Take time to study the history of the music you're playing.

72. Learn the lyrics of every song you play.

Chapter 6: Your New Musical Philosophy

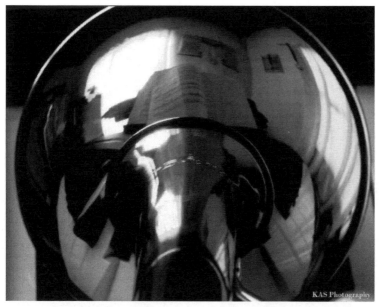

The reflection of the piano through a trumpet bell.
Photo Credit: Khadijah Simon

In order to access your full potential, there are things that you need to realize about yourself and about music. Most times, the way that you're thinking about it is exactly what is holding you back.

Your philosophy about music can either make it difficult for you to progress or easier than you ever thought it would be.

The bottom line is that music isn't hard. We just think it is, and then subconsciously put in effort to make it hard for ourselves without realizing it. Imagine if we took that effort and used it to work towards getting better!

Music only asks one thing of you, and that is for you to be ready (physically, spiritually) for it to come through you.

73. Don't aim to master music (or anything for that matter). You never will. If you knew everything that there ever was to know, you would be a master already. If anything, try to "master" learning.

74. It can't be impossible if other people are doing it!

75. Like water and electricity, music always flows the path of least resistance.

76. When the going gets tough, remember why you started.

77. Do not engage with musicians (or people) that don't have a growth mindset.

78. Never resist constructive criticism.

79. Do not make anyone make you feel that there are any boundaries to what/how you can play. The only boundaries that exist are the ones you decide to create.

80. Not everything you play can be logically explained. This is the magic of music.

81. Do not create any room for ego.

82. The music does not come from you, but it is influenced by you and everything around you.

83. Eventually, you will outgrow the people you play with and the venues you play at. There is nothing wrong with that.

84. Let there be a balance between music and all other areas of your life.

85. Being a good musician is not enough. Be a good person first.

86. All musicians are painters of sound. The audience's ears are our canvas.

87. Mindful players are better players. Practice mindfulness daily.

88. If you only play to try to impress everyone, then you will never achieve that goal.

89. Musicians always say that they play music, but music is no plaything.

90. Your audience puts food on your table. NEVER disrespect them or take them for granted. Always make sure that they leave your show in a better mood than when they came.

91. If you try to find similarities between playing music and other things that you do, it will make everything you do so much easier.

92. How you live your life is how you will play your instrument. If you rush in life, you will rush in music. If you drag in life...

93. The only way to get into "the zone" is by trusting yourself and then letting go.

94. Believe in your abilities. People can hear when you don't.

95. Be patient with yourself.

96. Never feel jealous of anyone else's talent. You will never be somebody else, and nobody can ever be you!

97. Music is medicine for the soul. Be mindful of the kind of medicine you're administering to people, and yourself.

98. You will find your sound when you stop looking for it and just play what you enjoy.

99. Give the music what it needs, not what you want.

100. Music can't hurt you, so don't be afraid of it!

Extra letters

These writings were handpicked to give you some extra food for thought as you learn to apply these insights to your music. Two of the writings featured were done by my late mentor, Bruce Skerritt, who was dedicated to making music easy and understandable for all his students.

One of the ways he achieved this was by identifying similarities between life and music. This was evident in his writings as well as in his method of teaching.

Being able to find similarities between music and other things is a useful trait to have because it helps you understand that **everything is connected in one way or another**. A realization in music can become an idea for cooking, or a whole new outlook for photography.

"Everything on this planet works off the same principles, but you have to look where it counts."
Bruce Skerritt, 1951-2022

On Classical Study (Khadijah Simon)

On the outside looking in, studying classical music always seemed to me like devoting your life to learning other people's music and performing it flawlessly.

The problem I have with this is that in many cases, the musicians end up playing a collection of notes, without being able to understand what they're playing or why it works.

I realized this while at a music camp with a really talented pianist.

During our breaks, he would sit at the piano and play some of the most gorgeous music I've ever heard, and then go on to explain that he doesn't understand 2-5-1s (even though he just played at least 3 in the piece) or how to improvise.

It left me dumbfounded. I couldn't believe it.

Chopin, Beethoven, and Bach were just a few of the musicians who were known for their composition and improvisational skills, so why is it a lost art now?

Classical study shouldn't be about regurgitating written music. It should be about learning and analyzing it and finding ways to apply these ideas to your own playing.

For jazz pianists especially, solo piano pieces provide a goldmine of voicings, chord progressions, and licks that you could apply in your playing.

So, the next time you learn a classical piece, analyze the chords and the movements. Check for melodic phrases that can be turned into jazz licks. Observe the voice leading and find songs that you can apply these concepts to.

That is what will make classical study worthwhile.

Playing What You Hear (Bruce Skerritt)

When we speak we don't speak nouns and verbs and adjectives and tenses and..... you get the idea. We speak IDEAS. Even if they come from someone else, you can't speak what you can't think. You can't express your thoughts if you don't have the vocabulary to express them. Conversely, you can have the biggest vocabulary imaginable, but it's of no use to you if you can't think coherently.

For example, you can learn every word in the dictionary and get twenty degrees in English, but you still need to learn how to fry an egg, as simple as it is, if you don't know how to. How often do you think of how to spell what you say while you are speaking?

The only reason language and writing were ever developed (guess which came first) was to pass ideas/information from one mind to another. New words and phrases are coined to express new ideas - the words don't come before the ideas/thoughts.

Music is no different.

Coltrane never played scales and modes and notes and..... again, you get the idea. He played IDEAS. He busted his backside to develop the musical vocabulary he needed to express those ideas, even coming up with his own "words" and "phrases" (licks?) to express them. He also busted his backside to develop the skills and stamina necessary to even get close to expressing them (can you imagine what must have been going on in his head, that he couldn't quite reach?).

A wide vocabulary doesn't necessarily make a good poet a good speaker, or a voice that is distinctive and pleasing. 'Trane, among others, had them all. Do you really think he was thinking of the names of the notes he was playing? We can analyze all we want now, but you can't analyze anything before it's played. Otherwise, you're painting by numbers, maybe composing, but certainly not improvising.

Playing what you hear is no myth. If you can't "hear" it (not with your ears - with your mind), you can't play it. In the end, though, we're just conduits. Music doesn't give a rat's backside who plays it. We just get put, or put ourselves, in its way. Like electricity, it will take the path of least resistance.

What you say is determined by what you think. Unless you say something that someone else has thought for you. In which case you're not really speaking - just talking. What you play is determined by what you think. Unless you play.......

Rehearsal vs. Practice (Khadijah Simon)

Believe it or not, these words aren't interchangeable!
They mean different things and once musicians realize this, there can finally be more clarity when it's time for musicians to come together.

Practice is done at home.
This is where you take your time to learn the material and make sure that it's ready for the **REHEARSAL**.

Rehearsal is when you meet up to put everything together.

The Old French root of rehearsal is "rehercier" which means "go over again", implying that you would've gone over "it" (in this case, the music) already, right?

Yeah, you go over it the first time at HOME!
That being said, do not come to rehearsal to practice. Come to rehearsal to rehearse and leave practicing at home.

Playing music "by ear" (Bruce Skerritt)

The concept of "playing by ear" has always bothered me. Do we "speak by ear" too? Music is sound. Speech is sound. You can't see it, smell it, touch it, or taste it. You can't play what you can't think. You can't say what you can't think. Well, I guess you can but it will be an incoherent drivel. You play and say what you think.

Organized, coherent thought - organized, coherent music and speech.

Mastery Is A Hoax (Khadijah Simon)

I'm almost 100% sure that at some point while learning music, you've been told that you need to "master" this before you can "master" that, but unfortunately, I am here to say that mastery is a hoax!

It is **impossible** to know absolutely everything there is to know about music or any other subject. If you knew everything there was to know, you'd be a master already.

Other than this simple fact, people are also figuring out new and innovative ways to solve problems every day. We see this in healthcare, technology, agriculture, architecture, and music.

This has been happening for centuries, and we won't see it stopping anytime soon.

The idea of mastery, as gratifying as it may seem, is unrealistic and shouldn't be one of your goals. We must learn to enjoy the process of learning music because, truth be told, we will never stop learning!

My personal goal in music has never been about mastery. It was always about being able to physically execute the ideas that I have in my head and being able to learn new things that will influence the ideas that I get.

If you make this your goal, I can assure you that your musical journey will be so much more fun and fulfilling.

Instead of trying to "master" something, aim to practice and retain something valuable each day!

What Does Practice Make? (Khadijah Simon)

Throughout my musical journey, I have always heard people say that practice makes perfect. But since I've gotten older, I've realized the hoax that perfection and mastery are so I stopped entertaining that saying.

Soon enough, people came up with the phrase "Practice makes permanent", but that makes no sense either.

If practice really "made" permanent, you should be able to stop practicing for two years and come back still being able to play what you were practicing at the same skill level, right?

We all know that that's not how it works. So I didn't entertain that one either.

I started thinking "What does practice really make?" and that's when it came to me.

Progress.

Practice makes progress.

It gets you closer to whatever your goal is. The more you practice, the more you progress.

It doesn't sound as cool as perfection or permanence, but it's the truth and the truth always wins.

The Music Spirit (Khadijah Simon)

Disclaimer: This is my personal philosophy and hasn't been proven as fact by anyone.

The "music spirit" is an omnipresent entity. It is responsible for everything around us that has rhythm and movement.

Right this moment, there is an unimaginable amount of music in the air waiting to be written down, waiting to be played, waiting to find the right vessel.

For musicians, it feeds us what it wants us to play once we open ourselves. We have to be truly receptive to start receiving.

I also believe that there are different levels to its presence, and when you can get into what some people call "the zone," that is the point where you are most open and in tune with what the spirit is giving to you.

We must all aim to maintain access to this space.

The Vessel Mindset (Khadijah Simon)

Disclaimer: This is also my personal philosophy and hasn't been proven as fact by anyone.

The vessel mindset is having the ability to see yourself as an empty vessel. Think of an empty container. There is an entity (the Music Spirit) out there that pours ideas directly into us.

I find that this kind of thought process gets rid of ego. The truth is, the music doesn't come from us. It is influenced by us- our experiences, what we practice on our own, the music we listen to, the pain we've been through, our moral compass, where we live, how we were raised... but it doesn't come directly from us. The spirit fills our vessel, and we get to express ourselves through that.

Just like water and anything else, music flows along the path of least resistance. We have to make ourselves available in order for us to receive anything.

You will not be able to achieve certain things if you do not have the technical facilities to do so. Practicing and listening to music helps us to open our vessels to more ideas that this spirit could share.

Why Is It So Hard To Improvise? (Khadijah Simon)

When you were born, you didn't come out speaking fluent English (or any English at all), but you were able to hear your mother talking even while you were inside the womb.

Maybe your first word was dada, and then mama, and then a few years later you started learning the alphabet. At this point, you'd have heard people talking every day of your life. Whether it was your family members, the radio, or the TV in the living room, you were always exposed to people speaking English.

(You may wonder where I'm going with this, but just hold on.)

Around the time you started school, you learned about pronunciation rules, vowels, consonants, nouns, verbs, and adjectives, as well as learning how to read.

Now you are equipped with enough understanding of the English language to start making your own sentences. Your vocabulary might have been small, but that was okay because you were still learning, and you still had people around you talking all the time.

As you continued to learn and grow your vocabulary, you began to speak with more confidence and eloquence. You might've said phrases or words that you've heard others say, but you understood what they meant and how they fit into your sentence.

The most important thing to note, though, is that throughout your entire journey of learning the English language, **you were exposed to it daily.**

You heard different people speak with different accents; you heard how they pronounced their words, you heard how they raised the pitch of their voice after they asked a question; and all of these things influenced you and the way you talk subconsciously, whether you realized it or not.

This is why it's so hard to improvise in music.

Although we may learn some of the "language" and become familiar with the theory behind it, if we are not listening to it and letting it influence us daily, it will take a lot longer for it to become as natural as speaking.

Think about when you speak. Do you think about how to spell every word you say? Do you think of what nouns you use in your sentences, or do you just talk, knowing that you're saying words that you understand?

This is the result everybody looks for in improvisation, but it is only achievable by immersing yourself in the language and learning how it works.

It doesn't matter if it's jazz, blues, or classical. The only way to expand your vocabulary is to continuously seek knowledge and allow yourself to marinate in the "language" of the genre you're learning, just like how you marinate yourself in English by reading stop signs while driving, listening to your friends vent, and reading this book.

Made in the USA
Middletown, DE
16 August 2024